Mambo Lips

The Memoir of a girl who found strength in being different.

By Joie Lamar

Copyright © 2015 by Joie Lamar
All rights reserved.

Cover design by Joie Lamar / Brainspired Publishing

No part of this book may be reproduced in any form or by any electronic or mechanical means including information storage and retrieval systems, without permission in writing from the author. The only exception is by a reviewer, who may quote short excerpts in review.

Visit my website at www.joielamar.com

Brainspired Publishing
A joint venture of Brainchild Holdings Inc. and INspired Media Inc.

Brainspired Publishing
Ontario, Canada
www.brainspiredpublishing.com

ISBN: 978-1-7774054-0-3

MORE BY JOIE LAMAR

Salsa Hips
Memoir Series, Volume 2

Sapphoetry
Balladry

Cuarenta y Nueve
Homage to Pulse Orlando
Curator & Contributor

G
Crime Thriller, Volume 1

See Whores
Crime Thriller, Volume 2
June 2021

Forward

By Antoine Elhashem

Toronto, Canada

Publisher and Creative Director, theBUZZ and PinkPlayMags

Joie Lamar is someone I admire. I am blessed to call her a dear friend, in the LGBTQ community, but what you are about to read speaks for itself and not those emotions. I LOVE Mambo Lips!

I met and her equally wonderful wife Natalie, through our involvement in business and the community in the Greater Toronto Area. We are all equally passionate about gay issues, so it is no wonder that our paths have crossed several times. We have hit it off famously and it was not long before Joie Lamar was involved in community causes that I was involved in as well. She knows how much I adore the shining light that she is. I have loved chatting with her about so many topics.

We have talked about our lives, history, upbringing, beliefs, dreams, and passions during our many drives to and from volunteer meetings. We have even occasionally reminisced about our similar wild days in different gay locales around the world. We have always ended those conversations so inspired by the beauty that we both see in what makes us, and all other humans who are; the complexity of one's experiences playing into how you feel and act and live life today. It made sense that Joie should take to writing one day.

I have been fascinated with Joie's stories. She has clearly had a very rich and colourful life, and I am proud of how that has happened the person who I adore today. To grow up in New York, the center of the modern world in the 70's, must have been such an experience. I love reading about the crazy family and community stories. This book is full of stories that made me shake my head and ask, "How did you survive?" but clearly these many vivid moments would shape anyone's personal growth.

It's clear that there are many more stories for us to read. The story reads comfortably like a diary and still interestingly personal. I have never visited New York so the first few pages alone were engaging. I know that New York is a big part of who Joie is and Mambo Lips feels, in part, like her love letter to that metropolis. It is an honestly written journey. Joie does not hold back including her funny and blunt observations. It is a wonderful memoir, faux or not, that you will find yourself devouring in one setting. Joie has always been a good storyteller, but I didn't know she was an equally fine writer.

I don't want to give away much more that this and rob you from the joy of discovering the many surprises. Mambo Lips is just like those long conversations on our many drives in Joie's care; engaging, fascinating, and quite often chuckle inducing. I am so excited that readers will get to experience those moments with Joie albeit a little bit jealous.

Dedication

I dedicate this book to my beautiful muse and wife Natalie, a most complex and witty human being in her own right, who finds the genius in my crazy.

You make me want to sing, dance, and create! You make me a better person.

~ Siempré,

Joie

Preface

New York is an incredibly amazing conglomerate of cities or boroughs to grow up in. Who I am today is not just defined by the memories captured in this novel series, but also by the rhythm of the five boroughs. Each imprinted differently on my soul. Each played a different beat for me, ultimately creating my *Born and Raised in New York* anthem. This anthem will forever be the background music in my life story.

Brooklyn gave me swagger. I learned the 'look good, feel good' mantra of most people in the county of Kings. This is the city where I learned to be 'fly'. I also learned to ditty-bop in Brooklyn. Ditty-bopping is an ego boosting bounce in your walk. It is not easily done. Too much and you're a thug or a clown, depending on your morals. Too little and you appear to be handicapped. There is an art to ditty-bopping.

The Bronx is the only borough name that requires a signal word. It is 'The' Bronx because it is worthy of note, according to the dictionary. It is a borough worthy of survival skills for sure. I was mugged at gunpoint in 'The' Bronx and I learned a very valuable life lesson. That being fly, dittybopping and speaking Spanish won't save your ass from a mugging in The Bronx.

You grow up in New York knowing that the people in Queens like to party. We called it "boogie down" Queens back then. The beaches in the borough of Queens were also quite beautiful back in the 70's. Combine that party rhythm with beautiful beaches plus some mood enhancers of that time and you have some of the best summers of my teen-hood. Pap was a water sport enthusiast and quite the avid surfer. He taught us all to surf as if we lived in Rio, Brazil or Rincon, Puerto Rico. His famous correlation: "Never forget that New York is also many islands". He passed on that love for islands and ocean and all that that entailed in Queens, N.Y. Rockaway and Riis Beaches in the borough of Queens are where I spent my youth shredding waves.

Staten Island is the southernmost point of the entire state of New York. It is serene, for the most part. Many parts of the island are reminiscent of the seaside New England towns of Maine or Southern New Hampshire. It has the least amount of crime of all the five boroughs. Although I am not privy to actual data, I attribute this to the number of Mafioso that live in Staten Island. Their homes, mothers, wives, and children kept distant from where they conduct business. They don't shit where they eat and have kept it safe for the rest of us. This island was home for me. The Verrazano Bridge entrance to S.I. on a warm sunny day is forever emblazoned in my heart. I recommend that you take that ride in a convertible, top down, with Frank Sinatra singing Summer wind playing on the CD player...*Like painted kites, those days and nights, they went flying' by...*

Chapter 1

SURVIVING EL CUCO

They say your very first memory shapes your life forever. If this is true, this all makes sense now. I was just barely over a year old when Mama thought it was a good idea to pram pool. She and her best friend Sally, at the time, put both of their precious little girls in one pram baby buggy for the day. The sun was shining, and life was good in Brooklyn New York in 1960, so I am sure it seemed like a good idea at the time. I don't know if it was a fad or if Mama and Sally were the pioneers of pram pooling.

    Bonnie was a large child. Twice my size and from what I can remember at 15 months of age, quite unhappy. She was also exceptionally white with eyes so light that even the sun caused her red eye effect, without a camera. Her towhead, like strands of gold dipped white silken threads made her look like what I would one day picture to be El Cuco, the mythological monster my parents would consistently warn me about at the dinner table.

On this day, Bonnie - El Cuco was restless in our shared buggy. I would later find out that she was sharing MY space. I remember becoming angry, in my twenties, for her lack of respect for my property on that day. But whatever happens in the baby buggy stays in the baby buggy, so neither Mama nor Sally knew that a rumble in the stroller had begun. Bonnie was comfortably seated under my hood. Her large head filing the space almost in perfect contour to the hoods shape. I, being forced into a hostess position by Mama, sat at the foot end of the buggy with a towel held to the hood with clothesline clips, precariously protecting my precious and less skulled brains. Even at 15 months I felt vulnerable and cheated of the pram's safety. Bonnie continued to be restless despite the comfort and considerations Mama had given her.

Why no one noticed this before the buggy was positioned alongside the story window is beyond me. Parked just next to the door, outside a smaller butcher shop in Brooklyn, our mothers left Bonnie and I to stare at each other in the pram while they shopped. My full-lipped pout when they looked inside the pram was a desperate and speechless warning to this foolish act. How could I communicate that Bonnie's large head combined with her movement was jeopardizing the spring action and thereby balance of the pram with me precariously two feet off the ground? An engineer in the making able to assess the danger of this situation but not able to express myself or move out of danger. Cursed!

It did not take long for Bonnie to move even more erratically once she lost sight of Sally. In one fell swoop the pram teetered and tottered as I tried to compensate for the loss of balance. I surfed this wave as best as a toddler could have without formal training but alas, Bonnies' large towhead leaned the baby buggy away from the store window to a point of no return. In slow motion we stared at each other, eyes like saucers, as the pram bounced on its right hand side to the concrete ground below. I had somehow managed to shove my body between Bonnies' scalp and the top of the hood just before we hit the sidewalk. This quick thinking action saved my life, I'm sure. We did not get hurt. There was enough baby fat, big head, and full lips between us to break our fall. I don't recall feeling any pain or seeing any blood but long before we felt our mothers pick us up in desperation Bonnie cried hard. She cried so hard that she cried for the both of us and hysterically so. I on the other hand smiled. Not only had I surfed and survived but even at that young age, I knew my pram pooling days with big head Bonnie, El Cuco, were over.

Chapter 2

PRAYING TO THE SAINTS

Did you know that King crabs grow as large as 10 feet across? Nothing could prepare me for the sight of one walking through my Grandmothers front door when I was just four years old and at 3:00am in the morning. Someone had banged on the door hard enough to wake me that night. We lived upstairs and Mamabuela had the in-law apartment downstairs in our family home in Staten Island. It was a treat for me to spend the weekend with her. So far, I was the only girl in the family, and she made me feel normal when 'girl' did not quite fit me. On this summer evening we had watched the Beverly Hillbillies while she explained all the saints, plants, incense, and oils on her alter. I was four years old and so fascinated with Mamabuela's voodoo. Santeria is an African slave influenced variation of Christianity. The saints had dual roles as entities that can influence your life or the lives of others, given the right spell and placement of feathers, beads, and or different foods. We prayed to them as Catholics, using their good Christian saint names, and danced around them to conga tunes using their African spirit names. My Mamabuela was the highest ranked Santeria in all of New York and she was convinced that I would carry on the legacy. Every weekend I learned more and eventually I earned my beads. These beads were always specifically coloured and arranged to keep my entity with me. Ellegua, or Saint Anthony, is my spirit saint but even he could not help us on the night of the king crab. My father came running downstairs only to find himself looking at the back of crab royalty as it walked into my Grandmother's apartment. I could see the shock on his face. Our eyes met and despite my young age I know that there was a mutual what the fuck? being telepathically transmitted between us. The crab entered with all the grandeur of a Japanese horror film. Slowly it lifted its front claws heading straight for Mamabuela. It filled the doorway coming in and it did not disappoint once it had a chance to spread.

It was red and white with a pattern that looked like flames walking to a four-year-old child who could not comprehend its existence in this space. Every claw clicked multiple times as it walked on the wooden floor towards Mamabuela. She was only 5'2" and I was smaller than her at this age. I didn't want to see her eaten by this creature, so I prepared to pounce just as my Grandmother's voice went deep. Not deep like she was angry and being stern, but man deep. I looked quickly towards my father for assurance. Should we fear the crab, Mamabuela or both? He came around the crab to take me in his arms just as my grandmother began her full-fledged voodoo routine. She spoke in tongue, a combination of Arawak & African. She danced around the king crab and dusted it with all sorts of beautiful colourful powders. Mamabuela put her hands on both my Papa's head and me and broke into what were both voodoo and a catholic prayer to protect us. We both had red ochre thumbprints on our foreheads where she was finished. The king crab watched her every move and snapped its claws in defiance. My fingers were in my mouth and I was drooling all over my father. Mamabuela repeated the same words over and over as she moved closer and closer to the crab. I can only remember that the words were rhythmic and soothing. Just when I thought she was close enough for the crab to grab and devour her, Mamabuela splashed the crab with rum and put her hands on it to deliver a killer twist to its main body. The rattled and dropped into a pile in front of her like a puppet whose strings had been cut.

Papa helped to sweep it into a very large green garbage bag and was given detailed instructions of how to dispose of it. Apparently, another Santeria or Santero in New York vying for the voodoo top spot had sent the crab. It was very powerful and evil spell. My father could not touch it at all, and it had to be placed far enough so as not to do further harm. Her directions were explicit, and she was very serious about how touching it could endanger him. My grandmother cried that morning like a woman drained and spent. I wiped away her tears and asked her to wash her hands. I was a four year old afraid for her and the repercussions of her touching the evil king crab to kill it. She reassured me for many years but then her pains started. Her pain would eventually be diagnosed as cancer. I knew one thing for sure upon hearing that news. I would never follow in Mamabuela's Santeria footsteps.

Chapter 3

LOSING GLORIA

The summer of '65 was a turning point for our family. Although Mama still prayed to pictures of Jesus on my sister Gloria's shrine, she didn't cry anymore. Papa had purchased a huge Chevy Impala stations wagon that he washed & waxed consistently. My brother and I knew this purchase were Latin parent speak for growing the family and the shirtless car wash act some sort of mating call. The fact that Mama giggled and swatted the window screen with her tea towel as Papa smiled from below spoke volumes about how truly healing this year was.

Gloria was two and a-half and I was just six months old when our Papa came home from work late one night. During the day, he worked for the legal aid society, saving the world and downtrodden as he often reminded us throughout the years. He had taken a second job that summer at the marina. Papa was cleaning up the charter & private fishing boats as they came in at the end of the day. My parents were saving up for a new and bigger car now that they had three children. My mother prepared his lunch at five o'clock in the morning that day. His favourites; spicy tuna salad with extra mayo, a thermos full of real coconut water and sliced mango for dessert. With two little once attached to Mama plus a six-year-old running around in cowboy boots looking to scalp Indians, my Papa left for work on the brightest morning of the darkest day in his life.

Everyone who worked on the boats would drop their dinner and beer in a bucket that would float in the colder bay water while tied to the dock. Papa took his 5:00am prepared lunch and did the same as everybody at 5:00pm that day. He had spent the entire day in the sweltering Manhattan courts filing paperwork for the many cases in his workload. It was a hot and steamy day, but Papa would not be satisfied until the only thing occupying space in his briefcase was that lunch. Too harried to eat, he made a mental note to cool it off at the Marina and enjoy the meal for dinner. Why stop for dinner and get home late on a Friday night? But once again his commitment to his work preceded my Papa's plans. Many private boats pulled into Atlantis Marina that night. Papa cleaned so many that he came home with a whopping $300! Who could eat with all the excitement of that wad of cash in his pocket? He was picking his new car colours in his mind as he pulled into the driveway at 1:00am in the morning to a chorus of babies crying.

Mama was exhausted so he did not get to give her the great news. Instead he was handed my unhappy sister, while I received a boob delivered milk shake after my Mother tried to breast-feed and rock a toddler at the same time.

Papa was so gentle and loving. I thank God that never changed even after this night. He sat Gloria on his lap and gently sang ballads to her while feeding her his spicy tuna sandwich. He made her giggle and filled her belly, a perfect recipe for putting her to sleep peacefully. He came back to the master bedroom, proud as a peacock and ready to tell Mama of the $300, only to find her asleep with me attached, sharing dreams.

The sound of vomiting is unmistakable, and all parents have extra kept hearing when it comes to their child feeling ill. Mama sprang up at almost four in the morning to find Gloria throwing up and convulsing. Papa called the ambulance immediately. She was burning up. The paramedics took her and my parents while my brother and I went to Mamabuela's apartment downstairs. She remained lifeless while still breathing for almost a week. My only sister Gloria died of bacterial meningitis because Papa fed her tainted tuna and mayonnaise unknowingly. I used to hide in the hallway and watch my father cry to her picture every June, on her birthday, and on all the holidays too. My Mother never blamed him but seeing tuna cans or jars of mayonnaise was like seeing the devil for her. Those foods were banned from our home and our mouths forever. He blamed himself until the day that he died.

And so, the hardest years of my growing up were from one to six years of age when my parents and brother were always so sad. I took it upon myself to be extra cute and funny. "Jojo, you're our funny angel" was the consensus. I like to think that I entertained them out of their Gloria funk and into the Impala station wagon sexy years. The family was planning on of our many drives down to Miami in this new automobile.

Chapter 4

PAPA IS AQUA MAN

We were so excited that we never really noticed my incessant cough. I was a sickly child and susceptible to pneumonia. I was diagnosed with my third bout just two weeks before the end of school in 1965. Not only had I ruined the family vacation but also now Mama and Papa were officially worried. Even Mamabuela joined us for our appointment at the new Nose, Ears, Throat and Eyes Hospital over the bridge in Brooklyn. This was a state of the art facility that I now realized looked very similar to the Museum of Natural History. It also had the same acoustics. I can't tell you how many times my ear was twisted simply because I tested the acoustics with a variety of jungle sounds. In typical South American and Puerto Rican fashion, we dressed to the nines for my doctor's appointment. The building dictated the attire, so churches and courthouses and hospitals such as this one warranted, we dress up. The doctors were creepy and scary back then. It was at least my experience that they didn't care to be otherwise too. I don't think bedside manner was a chapter in any of their studies in those days. Nurses were cut from the same cloth. They were mean and many hurt me as a child. I look back and think about how many of them I would have grabbed by the throat as a parent. But civility was very important to my parents. They would never want to appear otherwise. I think they were also numb and scared after Gloria's death. Now their funny angel was sick, and it could not have been easy for them.

Creepy doctor and his mean nurse scheduled me for an emergency tonsillectomy. Clearly this was the root of my many bouts of pneumonia. However, they explained it to my parents at the time made sense to them. The entire family brought me back for my surgery on Monday. Once again, we were overdressed.

"You will not remember anything, and it won't hurt a bit" were Dr. Creepy's last words before I was knocked out for surgery. Wrong on both counts, it is not a surprise that he botched this up altogether. I awoke in the middle of the night burning up and in pain. I could feel string taped to both corners of my mouth and my throat was raw. I dreamt of sleeping in Papa's arms while in a lounge chair, poolside, and at home. I needed to drink, and I needed to swim to cool off. I wet a cloth that I found on my hospital side table with water from a plastic pink pitcher found in the same place. I put that cool cloth on my lips and on my tummy. The night finally gave way to sleep.

A large shadow blocked out all the light over me that morning and startled me awake. It was large and in charge mean nurse and she was not happy with me. Apparently, the cloth and pitcher on MY side table was not for MY use. She was annoyed with my audacity and proceeded to rip the tape and string off my mouth before leaving in a huff. I was six years old and feverish to the point of defiance. I put the cloth back on my head to cool myself off until my parents arrived to take me home. I was so thrilled to see them both that I did not fuss about my crispy itchy dress nor did I tell them that I tasted blood in my mouth. I was sure both would go away once I was home.

Late that night I came to with my Mama putty clean pyjamas on me and surrounded by blood that I had vomited in my sleep. She kissed me several times and handed me to my Papa and grandmother. She could not bear taking another daughter to the hospital is what she would explain to the adult me many years later. My father and grandmother drove me back to the museum hospital. I managed to make some small tests of the acoustics as he carried me inside. Mamabuela smiled and made a chicken noise for me that sounded like a full coop under these vaulted ceilings. I was admitted that night and would remain hospitalized, with short trips home, for an entire year. I missed my entire first grade class in school, but Sister Mary Seamus came to teach me every day. Mama never came although sometimes I dreamed, she was standing and praying by my bed. Papa came often. Mamabuela would always come with him but wave from downstairs in the parking lot. That first night, I was placed in a breathing tent that would become a wondrous playground for me, thanks to Papa.

His handsome face appeared in between the heavy gauge plastic that I was enclosed in. I was six years old and I was scared. The tent was being filled with both oxygen and vapour, but my feat would not allow me to breathe normally. "Psst Jojo, I have to tell you a very important secret." "I want Mama" I replied with tears in my eyes. "She is coming soon but first I need your help." "What is the secret?" "Jojo, Papa is really Aqua man." I KNEW IT, I though, with a whale eyed expression! That was my favour cartoon on television, and I had pieced the similarity between my beloved Superhero and my amazing Papa a long time ago. They both could swim, dive, and surf incredibly well but it was all confirmed in my mind when my father came home wearing an Atlantis t-shirt from his job at the marina. Coincidence? I think not! And now I'm finally learning the details. "That makes you Aqua girl", he went onto explain, "which is why they have put you in this fish tank Jojo." "What?" Say no more, I'll be requesting a ride on that Seahorse pulled chariot as soon as I am out of here, I thought. Papa went on to ask me to put my arms up and back and swim, swim, swim every time I coughed, like I was doing the back stroke. It was the only way for Aquagirl to get better and again it was our secret. I didn't know it at the time, but my true Superhero was helping me to open my chest and lungs each time I lifted my arms up above my head. It was this action that made me healthier and stronger, but unfortunately something was still amiss.

As the adage says, the house turned into days, the days into weeks and the weeks into months. My health roller-coastered, while in the hospital, and one month before I was finally released from the hospital, they brought in a priest to give me my last rights. I had lost so much blood, which they attributed to several convoluted diagnoses that I received four blood transfusions' over two days to try and save my life. I was weak and frail, but I opened my eyes long enough to take it all in. It was a party for Aquagirl because everyone was there. Mama finally came. She looked swollen even though she smiled for me.

Mamabuela was there too, standing way in the back holding the most beautiful rosary of her vast collection, for such an auspicious occasion. Aunts, and Uncles and cousins all sat around looking at me with the smiles and wonder befitting a superhero. The priest smiled as he prayed in Latin at my bedside. Clearly Aqua girl was close to God. But it was my Papa who once again stole the show.

As it turns out, one of my little friends in the hospital was a toy heir. She was bed bound because of a critical blow to her head with a baseball bat. A family gathering accident that would leave her permanently blind in one eye. I made it my chipper little business to always visit Mary Katherine in her room, climb in her bed, and bring the play to her directly. We became close and our fathers became closer. Papa arranged for her father to bring a life size doll to my bed the night everyone was honouring Aqua girl. The doll looked like me and had a big pink ribbon pinned to her dress that read, "Hold my hand and walk with me."

"If these transfusions work, she gains her strength AND she can walk around again without incident in the next few weeks, we can send her home finally." These were the doctor's words spoken to my Mama and Papa earlier that week, which gave him the brilliant doll idea.

I will always be grateful for Mary Katherine's friendship and meeting her wonderful family while I was in the hospital. Our fathers remained friends for years to come. Mary Katherine went on to become a troubled teen who died of a heroin overdose in her twenties. She never came to grips with her blindness, or her scars. Ironically, my life size doll had movable eyelids and one would stick closed, so I named her Mary, after my hospital friend. I did hold her hand to walk right past the weak wobbly stage of such a medical ordeal and straight to my discharge home, almost a year to date of being admitted.

Two days after finally being discharged home, I once again vomited blood. Papa and Mama wrapped me up quickly and took me to the emergency room in the middle of the night. This time they were angry and less civil than ever. My father's voice echoed in the acoustics of the hospital like the superhero he was. I was weak but impressed. I could not hear the actual conversation, but I knew that they were explaining everything to this emergency room doctor in detail, starting with my tonsillectomy.

The doctor took me into his examination room with the kindness and confidence of Superman. I was scared but somehow, I knew he would be the person to end both my parents and my suffering. He wedged a medical device in my mouth that I would later learn is called a gag. This equipment locked my mouth and jaw open so that he could examine and work down my throat. With a nasal cannula supplying oxygen through two prongs in my nostrils, the doctor prayed my throat completely numb.

He went deep into my throat with his medical instruments and to my young horror removed what I could only describe as the smelliest ball of blood and tissue. It resembled the man-of-war jellyfish that Papa had told us to stay away from and I could only imagine that as Aqua girl, I had swallowed this creature whilst swimming. While my face was one of fear and disgust, the good doctors was one of great pride.

It turns out that the jellyfish was gauze they had left in my throat after my tonsil surgery. It was connected to that string that was taped to my mouth. The same tape and string that mean nurse had ripped from my little face without noticing that she had left something behind. For almost a year, not only was this gauze rotting in my body but also kept my internal wounds from healing. I was vomiting the blood clots that tried to form around the wounds and bleeding internally to the anemic state that almost killed me. Mama and Papa had every right to sue the hospital but not the energy. That Brooklyn hospital would eventually be closed because of many such mistakes. My parents would regret not suing for years to come. I walked away from the whole experience very strong and determined for a seven year old.

Chapter 5

MARI-MACHO

My parents became baby farmers after losing Gloria and dealing with my yearlong near death experience. Some crops didn't come to fruition however I had three new younger brothers by the time I was fourteen years old. I became quite the childcare expert with each birth. It's the Latino way for female children to become second mothers to their younger siblings. We also bear the burden of sharing in the household duties. It all began at the tender age of nine when I cared for a four-month-old infant full time during the summer, while my parents worked all day, and my older brother was charged with protecting the house. He took that assignment very seriously and went on to become a police officer as an adult.

My love for my baby brothers outweighed my discomfort as a girl child, thank goodness. I now know that I was trained to be maternal and that it did not come to me naturally. I should clarify that gentility and nurturing are not maternally exclusive. If anything, my Papa had the more natural tendencies towards these than my Mama. However, unlike most young girls, becoming Mommy felt foreign to me. It was thrust upon me.

I had started to play the "husband" in every game of house around six years old. I don't think that is unusual and I don't trust that therapists will ever know if it is, in my lifetime. What was different was my play of swooning my little friends before I proposed, and I was good at it.

I could transform myself to become a little Bobby Vinton with my long braid tight behind my head, changing into my brother's smallest "wife beater" t-shirt and lip syncing the song *'Blue Velvet'* into my hair brush like the most seasoned of drag kings. I brought the performance home when I followed the lyrics *'Warmer than May her tender sighs...Love was ours'* , with a kiss on the cheek. The crowd of two, sometimes three, went wild with that move. I became legendary as husband material during a healthy game of house under the domed money bars during recess at school, at an age when the little boys were not cooperative.

I stared at myself in the mirror dressed like this quite often, even when I didn't have my little girl friends over to play house. I felt so comfortable as a "mari-macho"; a name I was called often and meant to shame me, that even as a young child I wore it proudly. I would grow up to learn that it meant half-macho or half-man, but I bear no scars from that. I also embraced tomboy, dyke, and lesbo long before I knew I resembled those remarks.

My struggle was in accepting that I was a girl child expected to be thrilled about taking care of babies and playing real life house with my family's dirty laundry.

It was in an episode of 'The Fantastic Undersea Life of Jacque Cousteau' where I would find solace and an understanding of my true self. I watched Jacque Cousteau every week without fail, as any half mortal child of Aqua man should. Where else would I learn about the creatures that I would someday rule? I expected that Papa would someday test me, so I took notes. I was glued to this show since it was about Seahorses, the very essence of Aqua man's chariot, that I would drive someday.

This is the perfect time for me to inform any parents reading this that children teach themselves. The lessons are sometimes quite convoluted given their age, level of knowledge and what they are trying to sort out in those little heads. I didn't need answers as much as I needed to feel comfortable in my own skin. I had accepted Papa was Aqua man. With that came my thrill at being Aqua girl, apparently a mari-macho, but amazing just the same. But it was Jacque Cousteau's thorough Seahorse education that put me at ease with what others expected of me.

Unlike any other species, Seahorse males become pregnant. Females insert their eggs through an oviduct into the male's brood pouch. The male wiggles to get the eggs into position. Once all the eggs are inserted, the male goes to a nearby coral or seaweed and grabs on with his tail to wait out gestation, which may last several weeks. When it's time to give birth, he'll contort his body in contractions, until the young are born. He will care for his Seahorse brood known as 'fry' until they are old enough to leave to their own coral.

The lesson, to young me, was clear; that I could be little Bobby Vinton, a husband, and still be Mommy to babies.

I don't remember explaining this to my Mama as a child but many years later she gave me a gold Seahorse pendent as a gift. As beautiful as it was, I didn't understand nor remember the correlation to my childhood epiphany. "Thank you, Mama, but why a Seahorse?" I asked, "Because it is the only male animal that gives birth to its young," she replied. Click. Lights on. Lesson learned for two.

Chapter 6

HIP HUGGERS

I will never know if my masculine tendencies were ever the cause of an argument between my parents. They were both very subtle and gentle about "handling" me. Mama was adamant that I would never wear pants. The look on Papa's face every time he suggested a pardon let me know he was an advocate. I spent a great portion of my youth climbing, jumping, running and being quite the athlete with shorts on underneath my dress. The result, to Mamas chagrin, is my love for boy shorts and boxer shorts underwear today.

I was moved to tears when Papa took me downstairs to Mamabuela's apartment for the surprise unveiling one day. Mamabuela was a successful seamstress and he had commissioned her to make me my first pair of bell-bottom pants. The pants fit perfectly, which explained why my

Grandmother kept measuring every part of me for weeks on end. They were bright lime green, hip huggers, made from linen and with a big whit button closing on the one hip. The catch? They would remain our secret. Papa and I would go downstairs so I could change into my groovy clothes before he and I went out and changing back into a dress before going upstairs to my mother. Mamabuela had started an entire Joie clothing line by that point so I had many man tailored shirts to go along with my pants. *Hot fun in the Summertime* was the big radio hit and I was dressing like *Sly and the Family Stone*. How he managed to time my costume changes in and out of the house is beyond me, but we eventually got caught. Mama yelled, cried, and prayed but she was outnumbered. She conceded, providing the number of dresses in my closet exceeded my pants ensembles. I could never wear any pant outfits to church on Sunday. My parents went out and bought me a pair of jeans too. Her concession speech included strict rules about crossing my legs when I sat, regardless of what I was wearing, as well as being lady always like. I knew I was lying to her when I promised to abide by those rules but my craving for my "boy" wardrobe was strong. I did confess to Father Lang who suggest 5 Hail Mary's plus 5 Our Fathers for God to forgive my lie. Apparently, the closing itself was not a sin.

And so, it was that my new clothing unleashed the star athlete in me, bringing my older brother and me closer than ever.

The teenage boys played what was supposed to be touch football every weekend. Each of the teenagers had appointed themselves the Quarterback of a two-man team. Naturally, two-man meant a younger brother or male wide receiver to complete the team. My brother Cenzo bravely solicited me of course. I was fast and he could coach me in a different language. We confused the competition with our tri-lingual play calls since we spoke both Spanish and Portuguese. The advantage on all fronts put us in the neighbourhood two-man touch football championship game.

The pressure was on and the man-children playing were less than enthused about my making it this far. Cenzo was confident, cool, and collected. He still is that way to this day. The Fox brothers were mean on a good day. They fought often amongst themselves with Richie, the oldest, always beating up his younger brother in public. That did not make little Eddie Fox less aggressive. He had a mean temper and although I was taller, he was buff. He had both the face and temperament of a bar room brawler at just eight years old. He came to win, and he unleashed a verbal tirade that made my legs tremble. "Hey Cenzo! How come you came to play football with your dyke sister? Are you a fag Cenzo? May the Lame-ers are a fag family?" Eddie released. As I lost my temper, I lost my hearing. God knows I didn't understand any of the words he was calling us, but everyone was laughing. Everyone except Cenzo, and I could see the frustration in his eyes when I let Eddie Fox get the best of me. Cenzo had run in a touch down all by himself to tie the game in the fourth quarter. I was busy squaring up to fight Eddie, only to have him slam me in the mud while Cenzo scored. My brother called time out just when Eddie began to sing, "Joie is a creepy lesbian", bringing the crowd to a raucous laughter and giving Richie Fox a high five. It would be the last time that I would witness them unified as brothers.

Cenzo bent down and pinched my chin hard to get my attention. "Jojo, you cannot listen to him and listen to me at the same time" began my brother's speech. "Don't let them win in your head." "What is a lesbian?" I asked half whining. "Who cares? You're my wide receiver and you're doing a shit job Jojo."

My big brother was wise beyond his fourteen years of age that day, but he did go on to make me a typical teenager's promise. He vowed to beat both Richie and Eddie up if we won the game.

Revenge is still sweet at eight years old, so we dominated that last quarter of the game. Cenzo devised each play and traced it on my back while calling it out in the two languages that the Fox brothers did not understand. Eddie and Richie fell apart and turned on each other with each Lamar success on the field. My brother and I won the Clove Lake two-man touch football championship that year.

Cenzo did punch one of the Fox brothers in the face after the game but not because of his promise to me, but because Richie said, "now go home to your spic bitch mother" after the game was over. Eddie ran away before Richie hit the ground.

Looking back, my most profound yet simple conversation with my older brother took place on our way back home. He himself was bullied severely. My father's counter efforts to that bullying were atypical Latin measures of that era, so not very understanding or soothing. Thankfully Cenzo had developed a gentle and quiet strength as a result. He put his arm around my shoulders; smiling and said "We won Jojo. Good job." "And you know who lost?" he asked. "Who?" I replied with a huge proud grim on my face. To which Cenzo said, "Exactly!"

Chapter 7

WELCOME HOME AL

Most of my quality time with my father was either sports related or as his handyman apprentice. We spent hours upon hours in the garage working on a myriad of his projects. Am I a mechanic or master craftsman today? The answer is no, but what we did build was my confidence. "Can't is a lazy man's word and a limitation of the mind", Papa would say daily, from the minute you were born into the Lamar household until the day he took his last breath. It was not just instilled through his actions, but we were programmed to take anything on, and we did. He was a positive force in the family. A 'Can do' guy. Annoying to us, as we became teenagers, but brilliant once we were mature enough to appreciate him.

So, it was with some concern that we heard him say, "I can't remember where I put my shoes" for the very first time. Not because he did not misplace things but because he never used the words can't or cannot. The Papa we knew would have looked for the shoes without a word to anyone in the family. Another quality of my fathers was that he was as far removed from the word lazy as any human being could be. I don't want to insinuate that my Papa was the perfect man but only that he was an incredible role model, husband, and father. The saddest part of my childhood was to watch him degrade slowly over the years beginning with the first time he uttered the words I can't.

We would later find his shoes in the refrigerator. I was fourteen and Cenzo was twenty years old when Mama sat us down to describe what was becoming a pattern of forgetfulness for Papa. We had no name for what was happening, or any advertised reference to this condition back then. He was fifty-two years young and by all visible accounts in the prime of his life. Mama had just given birth to my youngest brother Gianni. Yes, it was late in life for another childbirth but to be fair the doctors had diagnosed this one as a tumour and treated it as such for six months. No one was more surprised than Mama to find out she would go on to name and raise this tumour, except maybe Papa. While sick and undergoing treatment, it had taken its toll on him.

Mama and Papa were undoubtedly soul mates. Madly in love since the day he told her she was too beautiful to be on her knees, even if she was praying to God, in front of a church in Recife Brazil. She was ten years younger than him and he was Puerto Rican. He was considered a different kind of Latino and somehow lowly on the plantain scale of spics. Some sort of Romeo and Juliet rift between families ensured but their love conquered all, even when her parents disowned Mama.

We assumed the stress of this medical issue was wearing on Papa and it progressively worsened long after Gianni came home.

All my brothers were beautiful babies. Gianni was a large tumour, I mean child. He weighed in a 10 pounds. 13 oz. and ruined our Christmas holiday. Mama went into labour on Christmas Eve, a Sunday, and was hospitalized where she remained until New Year's Eve. Gianni was born on Tuesday, December 26th, so we waved to Mama from the parking lot on the 27th. Everything remained under the tree untouched for Mama, Papa, Cenzo, the little ones and me. And by little ones I mean my four and two year old brothers, Xavier, and Lucien.

I spent my entire holiday vacation, off from school, taking care of the household while my mother gave birth and Papa began doing crazy unexplainable things. I became resentful for all these reasons and more but mostly because of my internal battle. Again, I know that today.

I prepared my speech for the next family meeting, upon their return. The one where I would let them know how this was the shittiest Christmas of my life. That same speech would include that I would no longer be at Mama's beck and call. I would tell her that I am not a slave, that it was abolished long before I was born. And finally, I would tell my parents to stop making children for me to take care of. If this went well, I would slip in that I am different and that they would need to accept that.

I practiced my speech in the mirror while trying to rock Lucien to sleep. He cried for 18 hours a day while Mama was in the hospital. Lucien was still breast feeding at two years old. I bottle fed an angry toddler during this time, but I digress. I was ready to assert my independence and stood strongly to that reserve until my parents came home and I laid my eyes on the tumour.

As I said earlier, all my brothers were beautiful babies, but Gianni cashed in on the gene pool. He had a biblical beauty, in my opinion. His beauty warranted cherubs flying around his bassinet. His thick long eyelashes and green eyes were mesmerizing only until he smiled, and then you fully melted.

I took my newest brother into my arms and never gave my parents that speech. He was my Christmas in 1972 and would grow up to be my best friend. Much would happen in between including Papa's progressive memory loss. He would eventually forget this Christmas and that this beautiful child was his.

My father was still working, surfing and energetic when they diagnosed him with Alzheimer's disease. The doctor did not expand on the disease except to discuss medication not yet appropriate for him and geared towards geriatric patients with dementia. We could barely say the name of his condition and decided as a family to call it "Al". My mother would often say that she is already for Al, now that he is home, jokingly. Papa remained confident and in good spirits in the early years.

Still, I decided I was not going to give in to my new feelings nor discuss them with Papa. At a time when most teenagers rebel, I wrangled my most recent awareness and confusion so that I could be a part of the family unit now looking after him.

Chapter 8

GOD FORGIVE ME

I was now quite sure that I was attracted to females. My intense, not necessarily strict, Catholic upbringing made me feel dirty about that attraction. I decided to find a religion that could explain my feelings. I needed God to send me a message through any one of the holy books that I was consuming at a rapid but in depth rate. I refused to denounce God, but like most teenagers finding their way, I admit to waffling with the concept of his existence. I filled my room with the many books of the bible both lost and published, the Holy Quran, the Talmud, the Torah, Zen, Tao, Buddha, and even the early writings of L. Ron Hubbard.

My parents never allowed any one of us any privacy, not even to study. Our culture dictates that privacy comes with paying rent or mortgage. I would have to squeeze this pursuit of religious truth in between crazy Lamar time. The weekdays were busy living in a loud and crowded Latin home, with only one bathroom. The weekends were filled with music and dancing. Mama loved her family dance lessons and sessions. The truth is we enjoyed them too. Mamabuela was an appointed dance judge and our goal was always to get her up on her feet for some serious old school salsa moves on wobbly legs. Papa listened to and collected every genre of music known to man. He loved his American Motown the most, but breathed salsa like it was oxygen, so naturally.

The little ones got away with free movement until they were old enough for her formal lessons. Mama's mantra was "the worst dancer is the person not dancing." She wanted us to dance through any inhibitions and I did. As destiny would have it Mama would teach me both to lead and follow when I danced. We were short on male leads, until the little ones ripened, and Cenzo was now a cadet in the Police Academy. He was not dismissed from the lessons altogether, but our teacher did allow for his "policing" classes. Cenzo would learn to lead and follow too so that we could cross train.

The big reveal of our talents would always happen at huge family summer pool parties at our Aunt and Uncle's house in New Jersey. Cousins from all over the world would join us for this unspoken competition. The adults cooked for days and the liquor was carted in by the case full. Every year we would learn either of a divorce, a separation or some family scandal that would dominate the kitchen conversation. This particular year my Titi Stella would be in the dance party spotlight for "walking out" on my Until Ionelli, as rumour would have it. More scandalous than that juicy tidbit is that she would attend the party with her new beau, an American black man. Tio, or Uncle, Ionelli was extremely handsome, gentle, and elegant. Titi Stella was beautiful, not to mention voluptuous and vivacious. The kitchen talk was all about the size of Stella's new boyfriend, respite with jokes and innuendos that I would not understand for many years. The smells and sounds of these parties are one of my favourite childhood memories.

Sandra put her towel down on the lounge chair and smiled at me from across the deck, causing our pool tag team game to go into slow motion for me. In seconds I was "it" and everyone around me was laughing and pointing. My new oversized bikini top had slid completely down below my nipples and my flat chest was bare for all to see. I can recall the 30 seconds of my subconscious not fixing the bikini so that she could see me bare-chested, right before embarrassment set in. All our clothes were purchased one size bigger than a perfect fit so that they would last an eternity. I was so thin and long at that age that I never truly benefited from the family business plan. Thankfully, Mama always carried around with back up for me from Cenzo's hand me downs. She came running over with one of his old 'A' t-shirts for me to slip over my bikini. Instantly, little Bobby Vinton was born again, and I had my charms set on my cousin Sandra. She had the power to slow down a game of tag and to speed up my heart. All my religious research was back home in my room. I would look for answers after this glorious party weekend.

Stella arrived with her new boyfriend Charles and my cousin Arturo. Arturo was an only child, rare in the Latin community, and spoiled beyond belief. He was also handsome beyond words, having come from such great looking parents, but he was the devil incarnate on a good day. Arturo never traveled without his high-end toys; mini-motorcycles, remote control airplanes, and pellet rifles – to name a few. Everyone flocked to him because of these gadgets, not because our cousin Arturo was liked, but because he was our real life Richie Rich. I kept my distance. Arturo scared me and he looked especially mean today as his mother introduced Charles to everyone. Charles was the epitome of class. He was well mannered and spoken and charming, judging by the ladies in my family swooning around him. He also tried to play with all the children throughout the day, including Arturo. He was fun and funny, but you would never know it by Arturo's face.

The sun began to set as we all finally rested, talked, and laughed around the dinner meal, featuring roasted pig cooked outdoors. Mealtime separated day play from the party. A hose lined up between two fence posts and pierced with multiple little shower heads became an outdoor bathing area for 6 people at a time. Children and women first, we cleaned up for the evening festivities. We could hear Papa playing his Motown and salsa in the basement. Everyone made his or her way downstairs to either the dance floor or the bar. My Aunt and Uncle turned on all the paper lanterns throughout their property as the sun set. The evening felt magical and the conga rhythms of the Latin music took over. Mama insisted we get on the dance floor with that quiet twisted face we knew to mean right now. Cenzo and I showed our training. We had turns and twists that warranted the awe. Most impressive was our ability to switch hit lead. My brother was badass, and I was smooth. We were also tapping the beer and liquor storage in the garage together. The beer high made me braver than normal and I turned out of Cenzo's hand to grab Sandra onto the dance floor. She didn't hesitate and held my open lead hand completely. We pulled in close to each other. She was beautiful and we were face to face. Her skin was the colour of caramel and her eyes, almond shaped and hazel. She had this amazing mole, like an actress of that time, right above the most perfectly shaped full lips. And she was sexy, even at only 14 years old. I also could sense this unspoken acceptance from her. Her eyes said, 'I know you're a girl, but I like you'. The people and family around us blurred as we spun like tops and moved to the rhythm. We became a vertical expression of a horizontal temptation. The poetry of the song playing warranted that I end this dance with a full on kiss. I pulled her close, leaned in and prepared to do so in front of the whole family when I heard the most horrifying shout. We all heard it and the music stopped to a scratching vinyl halt.

Arturo stood in front of Tia Stella red faced, crying, and screaming. "This nigger will never be my father" and "I hate you" he said loudly before running out of the house into the dark night. I was not as shocked by the word as I was by the hate in his eyes before he took off. Mama stood in between Sandra and me giving me that "we will discuss this later" face before she ran over to console Stella. Charles sat halfway on a bar stool, holding an engagement ring in his hand, but looking like he had the wind knocked out of his lungs. The men found Arturo many hours later. Titi Stella never married Charles. I don't know what became of him. Both she and Uncle Ionelli would spend their lives devoted to Arturo but living separate lives and alone. They never looked like a family again or even happy at family functions. I would get to kiss my cousin Sandra one day only to be completely underwhelmed. My dancing continued and so did my research for an answer from God.

Chapter 9

NORMAL IS JUST A DRYER SETTING

There was a lot of yelling and screaming about my mari-macho moves at the party when we arrived at home, but none were directed at me. My parents took my tendencies very personal. I hated the debates between them about who or what were to blame. Mama always quoted a bible chapter and verse that I have still not found, while Papa diluted it completely, calling it a phase. I was angry that my love for Sandra was more upsetting to them than Arturo's hate for Charles or black people.

I sheepishly made my way downstairs to Mamabuela's apartment in the hopes of speaking to her about it all. She insisted that we use the time to help me perfect my crocheting skills with yet another doily. Doily making was my

Grandmother's way of meditating. She had a knack for breaking out the crochet yarn and her many needles when she felt my stress too. We did not get specific about my feelings that evening, during our slipstitch and double stitch meditation session. Mamabuela did use this time to tell me one of her eye opening stories. It was strange at the telling but made more sense to me when I returned to my religious research.

She spoke about prehistoric animals. "Every animal that you see in the zoo today did not start as that animal" my Grandmother began her story. "Birds started out as land animals and much larger dinosaurs." "That's interesting, Mamabuela." I answered. I would have followed that with a bored snort and maybe rolled my eyes, but my Grandmother had no problem with slapping the snot out of me. "These dinosaurs that became birds" she continued "they felt like flying even when they could not." "Were you around with the dinosaurs Mamabuela?" I asked with a huge smile on my face. "Stop make funny and listen Jojo" she said in her broken English and unimpressed with my joke. We made twenty-four doilies that evening before I understood her story, although I did not apply it to my life at that time. The gist of Mamabuela's lesson, turned into a Joie metaphor was that *you don't give in to flying no matter how strong the urge, until you have walked sufficiently to realize you're not a land animal!*

I went to my room after dinner that evening to continue my research. I knew in my heart that God's message would jump out at me from any one of these books. Mama came in the room to find me sprawled on the floor with them and somehow assumed I was planning my future as a nun. I could not quite explain so I suffered through her explanation of celibacy and that nuns should not ever touch each other. I was right in the middle of the book of Job, so I had no choice but to be patient.

There it was, when Mama left the room, for my understanding - Job 35:11, *'who teaches us more than he teaches the beasts of the earth and makes us wiser than the birds in the sky?'* I went to sleep knowing that the message for that day was to take heed to fully understand Mamabuela's analogical story about how dinosaurs became birds.

The next morning Papa awoke more confused than we had ever seen him. I would come to understand that this was the natural progression of Al, but I blamed myself for distress on that day. I had broken him with my marimacho dancing, with a cousin no less. He would have never argued with Mama about it either. Cenzo solidified my guilt by not speaking to me that morning. It would turn out that he was upset about my out-dancing him that weekend but in my mind, I was responsible for Papa's decline. Mama needed my help more than ever. I took care of all my baby brothers without complaint and fixed dinner too. It was summer and everyone my age was at the beach that week. I took on the kids, the laundry, and the meals. Somehow that was not enough to melt away the guilt, so I decided to "walk even with the great urge to fly." When I finally did make it outside, to the beach and to surf I look at boys differently. They had always tried to talk to me, but I didn't know how to respond to another Bobby Vinton, and frankly they were not so smooth. I was determined to figure it out for Papa's sake.

Alex was dancing on the beach when we first saw each other. They had built a dance floor, eight feet by ten feet, on the beach and made from wood. It was dug out and perfectly level. A dusting of sand on top made it easy to turn and dance with dry bare feet. He was seventeen and three years older than the new 'walking' me. He was half Japanese and half Puerto Rican. It was the Latin half that made him suave, but it was the Japanese half that attributed to his tall Bruce Lee good looks. Most important was that Alex was a great dancer. He taught me how to dance the hustle on the day we met. I, unintentionally, taught him how to fear a wave. He also had a car, a bitchin' Datsun 240Z. If I was going to try and assimilate, and be "normal", Alex was the perfect guy. He was not brilliant, but he was decent and nice. My parents and Cenzo loved him so much that he visited with them even when I was not home. Alex and I stayed inseparable for more than a year. We won many dance contests together. He gave me my first kiss and when I turned down more than that, he still gave me a ring. But his greatest gift to me could be seen in my parent's eyes.

As horrible as it may sound, Alex and I parted ways because he tried to convince me that I loved him, and he was too nice. I did not want a bad boy, which would have caused my parents to worry again. I was looking for a boy to stimulate my mind and emotions like many girlfriends did. I could not share this dilemma with anyone at the time. Instead, I told Alex he was smothering me on the day that he gave me that ring. He picked me up from basketball practice to all my friends' excitement in his crazy cool sports car. I did not know this at the time, but he stopped to speak to Mama and Papa before coming to get me. He solicited and received their blessing to give me a promise ring and to propose to marry someday. My parents were understandably disappointed when we broke up, but I made them happy by parading several possible male suitors through the house. My boyfriends were every colour, every shade, and every nationality. Some stand out as truly brilliant and nice young men that any girl would be proud to call her boyfriend. Other? The typical waste of time and not worthy of type in this memoir.

By chance, Willie and I partied in much of the same circles. Our eyes met on several occasions, but I was too cool to give him the time of day. At this point in my life, I was a little truer to myself, and going both ways. I was almost seventeen and focused on becoming a professional surfer, artist, or Aeronautical Engineer, depending on the strength and origination of the marijuana I was smoking. I still felt dirty when with a girl due in part to attending an all-girl Catholic high school and the baggage that comes with.

Let me insert here that I do not resent my Catholic upbringing in the least. We as humans have bastardized it all to justify our propensity for hate. Enough said on that subject, but it did cause me more confusion with my Lesbianism at the time.

I was still deeply involved in my research and now reading the sacred texts of Tao Te Ching. So imagine my surprise when this shockingly pale young man with green eyes and very long hair, wearing a cape, approached me to say "I'm here because in order to get what you want but you don't have, you have no choice but to venture outside of your comfort zone." I had just read that same line in my research the night before. I attributed it to serendipity, young and naïve as I was at the time. The truth is our mutual friends were trying to set us up and fed him the ammo. He was different and the word metro-sexual had not yet been uttered but he truly embodied the word during our courtship. Willie was much more like a woman than any man I had ever met. We clicked intellectually and spiritually so the physical followed although still quite unnaturally to me. I confided my confusion and dual life to him one evening, under the influence of course. It was a time of sex drugs and rock & roll after all. For the first time in my life I heard words of acceptance and kindness. They were marijuana induced, I know, but Willie made the dirty go away. I was so emotionally needy for this deep conversation, with anybody, that I may have mistook the understanding he showed me for falling in love. I certainly did not appreciate how enlightened we both were at the time of our age. We became a couple and I stopped thinking about women when we became pregnant. I was eighteen years old and Willie was twenty-six.

My life changed with my pregnancy. I was now a Seahorse again. I continued to go to my parent's house in Staten Island to take care of my Mama, Papa, and brothers. My maternal juices kicked into overdrive. I stopped doing anything that could harm my baby. I became serious about keeping our home and my university education. School was in New Jersey. We had a beautiful Manhattan apartment on the upper west side. How I made it between these three locations, so far from each other, to manage my life at the time is still a mystery when I look back. My energy and strength, both mentally and physically, was endless at the time.

Willie on the other hand transgressed. His creativity and work suffered. He was a budding Claymation artist, ahead of his time, with many contracts in queue. I will never know how the pressure of all that happening so quickly could turn him from metro sexual to a macho pig, but it did. Life should not change your character and we had both read enough books to keep it together.

We fought constantly and it became clear to me that this normal was not my normal. Willie began to delve in the cocaine culture of that time. Our son was born in November, two months shy of my nineteenth birthday. Willie showed up at the hospital high and drunk and I had him removed by security. Our baby was now the only thing in our relationship that I was grateful for. I tried to make it work for our son's sake, but I moved out, with Cenzo's help a year after the baby was born. Willie showed up high and tried to change my mind by hitting me into submission. Cenzo nearly killed him when he found us fighting.

We came to grips with what had happened once I moved out. I met with Willie at a café in Greenwich Village to discuss that I only wanted child support to help me with our son, while I was still attending university. I was in the Electrical Engineering program and had already secured a position with AT&T.

While he pretended to be mature, kind and understand I could see Willie was high. His Cuban bullshit vocabulary always kicked in when he was high. I had high hopes that this was a phase and that he would someday have something to show for the brilliant man that he truly wan, if only for his son. That hope would transfer to my baby boy, just six months after Willie and I parted ways.

I had just received my paperwork from family court defining my child support payments, to begin in fifteen days form the date of the letter. It was one hundred dollars a month. Not a lot of money even in 1979 but enough to have Willie exercise his father muscle more than just stupidly calling to speak to his infant son.

We did not have call waiting back then so I was sure it was him calling on that Sunday morning to discuss the same paperwork. He was cc'd according to the documents. Instead, I found myself talking to a mutual friend of ours who used to live in our same apartment building back in Manhattan. "Have you seen the news or newspaper yet?" She asked. "No, why would I, I'm studying, and the baby is teething" I replied. "You need to Joie. Willie was killed." I can't remember what I felt on that day. I was numb and I tried to refrain from exhibiting any kind of emotion that my son could feel. I know that my life with Willie poured over my head like a water fall of snapshots, pictures of happy moments appearing in the water. I still had a slay figure he had made me of a pregnant Kangaroo that now was in my son's room. That flashed brightly in front of me. I gathered myself, and my baby, so that we could take a nice walk in the stroller to the newspaper stand. There I found the story and his picture in the little circle along with many others killed in a drug raid in Queens that Saturday night, on the front page of the New York Post. Willie was a social cocaine user at best, even if he was using too much. He did not have the heart or street strength to be a dealer. The police finally came to give me the news. Cenzo was there with me. I cried for my son who would never know his father and I cried for my enlightened friend who somehow had lost his way.

Several months later the investigation would prove that Willie was not only just a small user but truly in the wrong place at the wrong time. It would also disclose that the police and not the drug dealers had killed him.

I would never know what it is like to receive child support.

Chapter 10

OUT AND ABOUT

Wepa is the Latino word for woohoo. It is a word that expresses happiness derived from freedom. Freedom begins in your head. Scratch that last sentence if you are in a hostage or slave trade situations. What I mean to say is that I started to hear my mind shout wepa the minute I became happy with myself. Wepa is also a mating call. When you hear it in your head, people see it on your face and the rest is magic. I embraced the word and me fully.

I don't mean to imply that Willie's passing resulted in my freedom, but it certainly closed a chapter in my life. I would not reread the straight book ever again.

My new story led to some great gay and lesbian friends. I was amazed at how many of us were in New York, let alone the world. This discovery led to my shelving all my religious books and writings. I quickly deciphered that Gods message was right in front of me. It was in the people I was meeting, the places I was going, and it was in the beautiful lesbian clubs throughout the city. I concluded my research but gained my spirituality because of all that I read.

Every experience in my life had culminated to serve this out and about Joie well. Pretending to be Bobby Vinton for so many years gave me great confidence. Mama's dance lessons made me brave. Dancing salsa with Cenzo and the hustle with Alex made me a talented dancer. All this, tempered by my natural shyness, made me a pubic hair shy of cocky. I shed the long braided hair and started to dress for me. WEPA! I had never felt so authentic! This is not a self-help book by any means, but I recommend that everyone seek to be their authentic selves. It is liberating, comfortable and soothing like a lavender scented warm bath. I would imagine it is the same feeling that baseball players get when they scratch their balls right in front of eighty-thousand fans.

One small detail would derail the butch train that I was now on. I did not understand women. Don't yell at the book, I cannot hear you. I am very aware of my gender, but I don't necessarily click with all of it mentally. There are many reasons for this, but again, I am not a psychiatrist. I grew up in a male household, took care of male children and was never a feminine girl. I connected with my father growing up. The reason why was not as important as the dilemma.

Pure females as I call them are sensitive, calculating and oh so complicated. I could write a War and Peace size novel to truly describe a pure woman, but let's just say those three traits threw me for a loop. Some women use their beauty and sensuality for evil. I know no creature on this earth with so many dimensions like a woman. I would like to say that I enjoyed the on the job training, but it would be more honest to say that I am glad that I survived. I was certainly dedicated to the cause.

The Sahara was one of the most elegant lesbian clubs in New York, of that time. It was owned and run by a fellow butch who may or may not have been involved with the Cosa Nostra. I will not speak ill of the dead, but she did want us to think she was a gangster. I began working at the club every other weekend to supplement my income, providing Papa was well and mama could babysit for me. I was a barmaid. Hired because the owner's lover was interviewing the day I came in for the position and because I could dance with the drink tray on top of my head. Surfboard balance had finally paid off. We were required to wear a tuxedo shirt, cummerbund and bow tie to work. It was a uniform that the rest of the staff abhorred, but that I loved. The gangster owner dressed in a different tuxedo every weekend. She complimented how crisp I looked and assigned me to the front room on my very first shift. The font room of the Sahara Club on east 82nd Street in Manhattan was my golden goose. Yes, this applied to the money I made as a barmaid too, but my reference is really directed to the type of women I was meeting, and all that I was learning every weekend. The more mature and professional crowd loved that front room. Many super models, judges, attorneys, entertainers and more graced Joie's room, as I had taken to calling it. These ladies dressed to the nines and ordered drinks like *Courvoisier and Remy Martin*. Each of them liked these drinks served a certain way. Some of them liked to talk, some wanted a hug when they arrived, and some wanted to feel important. It did not matter the scenario, I remembered their names, likes and dislikes.

I would finish my shift in the front room one hour before the club closed altogether. That was my time to go upstairs and dance. I was young and naïve. Having the dance floor clear to encircle me while I hustled to Frankie Valle's *'Swear to god'* or Tavares' *'Heaven must be missing an Angel'* was my fifteen minutes of fame back then. She interrupted my game with a smile and a wink from across the room. I tried to wink back and not only lost my step but managed to hit my dance partner in the head with my elbow. You can easily recover from a funny awkward move when everyone is dancing with you, but I was now the spastic show in the middle of the circle.

Lisa introduced herself with the best line ever. She said "Hi, can I help you with that seizure you just had?" It was embarrassing but I am attracted to sarcasm. Not mean but intelligent sarcasm and specifically intelligent sarcasm with amazing beauty. She was all the above.

Our dates would be confined to the club. It seems like our schedules could never sync up, the weather, emergencies, my son, school and maybe just maybe Lisa was just a weekend lesbian. I was comfortable with what I called our Sahara relationship. I was at my best in this environment. She was comfortable behind the club walls.

Lisa was my first profound female kiss. We danced, we laughed, and we thoroughly enjoyed each other in the safety of the Sahara Club.

Nothing I had imagined could live up to my first female kiss. I pretended it would be my last kiss to give her all of me, a ritual I still relay on today. I breathed her in completely with each turn of our heads, lips, and tongues. Somehow our heartbeats synchronized. WE were gentle with each other, slightly embarrassed in public, but we would go on to kiss many times.

Eventually we grew apart. I fully embraced my sexuality. She found her happiness with a man and had several beautiful children. I would receive a note from her, years later, in the mail. It read…simply…"You set the bar."

I mentioned earlier in this chapter that I discovered women are complicated creatures. Lisa would be my first lesson into unraveling some of that mystery. Guess what world? A lesbian relationship is just like any other, for those wondering. It is never about the sex. It is about a connection, our ability to match rhythms, soul to soul. This I learned in a club on east 82nd Street in Manhattan.

Chapter 11

LOS DOLORES

I am blessed to have such great female role models in my childhood. Mamabuela shaped my life in a multitude of ways but I have never given my Mother her full share of credit until this writing. She is a force to be reckoned with. She worked late hours as a cashier, wherever she could get the work, and took great care of four young boys, including my son, during the day. She retired from Wal-Mart after seventeen years of service. When she did have any chance to really rest, she would cook instead. I did not appreciate all that she did when I was a teenager. Huh? Imagine that?

Mamabuela was some help, mostly with the kids, but she started to complain about aches. The aches turned into sever pain and she became a recluse in her apartment. Papa would still visit and sit with his mother often. He never lost cadence with that profound love. He did lost patience with her constant crying, mostly out of frustration. The doctors could find nothing in the multitude of tests that they took. "Old age is painful." Mama would say to her. My Grandmother took to sitting on the radiators in her apartment to relieve the pain. I would find her there many times, crying alone. "Jojo" she said to me one day through her tears "No one believe me, but I know I have cancer." "Please don't talk nonsense Mamabuela." My sadness for her was almost too much to bear. "I do Jojo, I know I have cancer." She went. "I need you to promise me that you will make sure that the family lets me die with dignity."

I made that promise to her and I still don't know if I kept it. When does wanting to keep someone who is so amazing alive become undignified?

The community called her Doña Lola. Doña is a title of great reverence. She was one of the most selfless people I have ever known. She volunteered to help every cause and remained dedicated to many even when in serve pain. I think her most profound history is that my Grandmother would take a day to travel all around her country, once a month, giving money to my Grandfather's mistresses for their children, born of that infidelity. Many of those children would grow to know her and love her like a Godmother. Lola was a nickname for Dolores, her first name. Ironically, the name Dolores means pains in English.

My great Uncle Rafael would eventually find a doctor, in a private hospital, that would discover Mamabuela's colon cancer. He had the money to pay for top-notch medical care. We would all be shocked by the diagnosis. We all swam in the guilt of thinking it was in her head or just old age for so long.

She was of course in the later stages. The first medical step was a colostomy whereby they removed the cancerous part of her colon and sutured the healthy end of the colon to her abdominal wall, outside of her body. She came home wearing a belt and bag over that opening where she could now poop in. The doctors were very meticulous about diet and a regiment that she would now have to adhere to keep the bag from overflowing. She no longer knew when she was pooping. The whole process disgusted my very proud Grandmother.

Mamabuela went into a deep depression and did not follow any of the doctor's orders. She wanted to leave this earth enjoying her food and the amount, both of which were against orders. The saddest part of her ordeal was that she felt that she always smelled. She often did. I still carry the guilt of telling her that she stunk one day. It was supposed to be playful, and I really did forget the bag and her complex, but you can never take back hurtful words. I made my wonderful Grandmother cry. I have apologized so many times both in life and in death.

Papa had left the house to pick her up from the shopping area when the doctor called. Her last checkup revealed that the cancer had spread to what was once her healthy colon and beyond. She would be hospitalized immediately for radiation and further treatment. My father was on his way to get her because once again her bag had overflowed in public. She was crying and already resigned to die when we gave her and my father the doctor's message.

We remained optimistic throughout the two years that Mamabuela was in and out of the hospital. The radiation turned her into a frail little bird, but the entire family chipped in to buy her a mink coat and a Daniel Boone fur hat, to keep her warm. She wore that consistently over her pyjamas in the hospital and whenever she was home for a reprieve.

You could feel the jubilation when you pulled into my Aunt and Uncles driveway when she came home that first Christmas. Drinks were flowing and the food smelled so good. We sat Mamabuela on the lazy boy next to their Christmas tree, dressed in her fur of course. She was so cute and so happy. We all knew that she would have to go into the hospital again but having her here gave us all hope. I held her hand after our big Christmas dinner and she said the same words she would say to me almost every day of my childhood. "You're special Jojo." "Don't ever forget that." In that moment I could feel her connection to God, spirits, and heaven, so I turned away. I looked away so as not to get caught up in one of her Santeria spontaneous embodiments, but I will never forget that feeling.

Mamabuela went back to Trafalgar Hospital, a beautiful private hospital in Manhattan, where she would remain another year. Her Doctor, Dr. Levine, was dedicated to sending her home to us permanently. He knew the entire family and showed my Grandmother such love during her care. There were times he would join us in her room to laugh and reminisce. Papa never missed a visit with his Mother. It was extraordinary to see them together.

She had a private, substantially large room in the hospital, thanks to my Uncle Rafael. We would often find church choirs in her room, singing and praying with her.

My father was visiting with her on the night of December 15th. They had just hosted a few cousins from out of town who had come in for the holidays to see her. She was weary from the long day of visitors when they left. She asked us all to leave but Papa stayed behind a little longer since I had a car.

We were expecting her home, just like last year, so I detoured to my parent's home to pick up the baby. Corey was asleep and warm on a cold winter's night in Staten Island. Mama asked me to stay and help her with gift-wrapping while we waited for my Father to get home. I wrapped our gifts for Mamabuela myself and put them under the tree. Papa called to tell us that she had asked him to leave too and was now sleeping anyway. There were no cell phones back then, at least not for ordinary people, so both Mama and I jumped when the phone rang. It was almost 10:30pm and Papa should be walking through the door at any minute. I knew what I was about to hear as soon as I heard Dr. Levine's voice. I was holding a bright red gift bow in my hands. She went into distress minutes after my father left the building and died that night. Papa walked in just as I hung up the telephone and I crudely should it out. "She's dead, she's dead Papa!" I could hear him scream "Nooooooo" into my neck as he fell on top of me, taking us both down onto the bed, sobbing uncontrollably. The entire family remained numb and civil straight through to her burial. More than a thousand people came to her wake and church service. My father covered her casket in a blank made of white roses. He fell to his knees and bawled like a baby, several times at the funeral and again at the gravesite.

We went through the holiday motions later that month without any tears, especially for the kids.

I faked my "ho ho ho's" and put on the Johnny Mathis music at my parent's house just like we did every year.

All was going splendidly contrived until Mama pulled out a gift meant for Mamabuela. I would start to miss her at exactly that moment, and I have never stopped. I realized, once my head cleared, that this was the shittiest Christmas ever.

Chapter 12

MAMBO LIPS

I would assume that because our body functions in the background of the rhythm of our heartbeat, even the brain relies on a cadence and not just blood flow. This is how I explained Alzheimer's disease to myself, when the world did not yet know enough about the illness. I imagined Papa's brain losing step much like I did at the Sahara club when Lisa winked at me.

We had gone through the gamut of homespun therapy along the way. Mama was very patient with my father. Cenzo managed to arrange his schedule to help her with him physically. Papa had started to become enraged at the moments when he felt we did not understand. He also broke many items in the house, confused about their functionality. I tried to figure it all out logically for the family. My first success was with labeling the appliances.

I was home when he began to get lost in the stories surrounding family pictures on the walls at home. What was once a soothing talk, simply reminiscing, was now like a record skipping. I replaced the old pictures with more recent photos so that he would stay in the now with us more often. It became more and more difficult to counter his episodes.

I started to keep Corey away from his Grandfather; often leaving him in the care of my sister in law anytime I would visit my parents. On of Papa's most disturbing personality changes, because of this ugly disease, was the amount of profanity he spewed during just a few seconds of confusion. God bless Mama, she would be called every disgusting insult and in three languages no less. Sadly, I decided this was no longer an environment for my son if I could help it.

My brothers would grow up immersed in his wrath as the disease progressed. It is the most heart-wrenching real life movie to watch a man who has been such an amazing father slowly become a monster to my siblings. Xavier was somewhat exposed to his goodness however those memories erased with time. Cenzo may have suffered some first born parenting mistakes. Lucien and Gianni only knew a life of terror with Papa. I was the only child blessed to have experienced the best Papa of his mind. Ironically, I was also the only child that was the spitting image of my father, mambo lips and all.

Mama's only breakdown was when Papa became adamant that Gianni was not his child. I can only imagine her shock at the fear on my baby brother's face when my father would scream, 'Who the fuck are you?" as Gianni entered the room. This happened more often with time, but Gianni became more resilient each time. He ran and swam faster than any child I have ever seen because of avoiding my Father's angry confusion. The story of this child became more convoluted as time went on. Papa was an identical twin. My Uncle Al in New Jersey was his mirror image. The joke between the two couples, back in the day, was that the wives could switch if either of the men because impotent. Papa remembered the joke and that my Aunt Margaret had laughed about it, but he did not remember the tumour.

With Mama's misdiagnosis, treatment and eventual birth over the Christmas vacation wiped from his memory banks, he was convinced of an affair that produced Gianni. My Aunt and Uncle visited alongside the doctor to help both Papa and Mama cope. He was eventually prescribed Lithium to temper his aggression. Mama became dependent on the drug for him. She could no longer live with Papa in between dosages.

I drove into my parent's driveway singing out loud and fully embracing Donna Summer's *Bad Girls*. My mouth remained agape as I looked up and saw Papa holding my baby brother over the second floor balcony banister. Gianni was pale and urinating on himself as Papa screamed incoherently into the house through the balcony doors. Cenzo pulled up in his patrol car and in full police mode. I ran upstairs while he moves my car and stayed under Gianni in the driveway. I could hear him calling for an ambulance as I ascended the stair to my parent's living room, two steps at a time.

Mama was on her knees begging my Father not to hurt the baby. The boys were crying backed up against the door. I yelled for them to go outside with Cenzo. I tried to convince Mama, but she would not budge. She was crying herself into some sort of asthma attack and I feared for her health.

I turned to witness the unimaginable up close. My Papa's veins bulged from every part of his head. Both of his hands were trembling as if they were opposed to his actions. "Papa, it's me Jojo" I said. "Please don't hurt Gianni Papa, I love him." His reply was garbled. "I am going out there to help you Papa." "You don't want to hurt the baby." I felt like I was addressing a stranger. Perhaps my mind was protecting me with that thought. My Father moved in closer to the sliding glass doors and me as I approached. A late dosage of his Lithium would soon be taking effect. That did not change anyone's fear of Gianni being release from the second floor, even with Cenzo on the ground to catch him.

I saw Gianni put his toe on the wrought iron banister. God bless my brother; he did everything to survive Papa back then.

I brushed my hand against Papa's shoulder. It was enough of a touch to have him look in my eyes. I'm sure he saw the love and pain too. That second of consideration allowed me to grab Gianni's shirt with both hands and throw him back over my head with every ounce of strength. He rolled and practically landed in my Mother's hands. She took him in her arms and ran downstairs. The ambulance had arrived during what seemed like an eternity to us.

Papa was looking at his empty hands and more confused than ever. He was still on the balcony, so I put my arm around him to bring him inside before the Lithium kicked in. I looked over the wrought iron banister to see Mama and my brothers being looked after. Cenzo was still looking up at me when everything suddenly went black.

My Father would have a psychotic reaction to the combination of medicines the doctor had prescribed. Adding Lithium to this prescriptive nightmare made matters worse. The confusion and memory loss caused by his disease was now the fuse to this dynamite mix of meds.

Papa grabbed my head from behind and slammed it to the wrought iron banister with such force that he broke my jaw and knocked me out. My face swelled to keep my lower mandible from completely detaching from my skull. I also suffered a concussion, lost some teeth, and will forever have a kink in my neck to remember Papa by, as if I needed it. I'm very grateful for not being awake when the police, including my brother Cenzo, swarmed the balcony to take Papa down and restrain him. I understand from Cenzo that it was so completely surreal to think his Father had killed his sister. I also know that my Father was incredibly strong in this state and they must have hurt him.

I was hospitalized for three weeks and released with my jaw wired shut for nine more. It was a gruelling hospital stay but not as painful as worrying about my parents and family. Papa was admitted to a full care facility that Mama would visit every day for nine more years. We never expected a breakthrough, however we prayed for him to recognize Gianni as his again. Just once before he left this earth. It never happened, so I made it my sister duty to tell Gianni all about the wonderful Papa he never got to know. He was fifteen when our Father died, and I don't think my stories softened his feelings. He loathed our Father.

Papa died on the very date that we lost Mamabuela, on December 15th, and almost at the same time. I found some sort of peace in thinking this was a heavenly plan.

My heart broke for Mama who lost the true love of her life. They were inseparable and a shining light of love together. She lived in darkness for many years after his death.

Everything I am today is because of Fabian Lamar, my Papa, or as the world knows him...Aqua man.

And by the way, the December of his passing remains my shittiest Christmas.

Chapter 13

SON OF SAM

Bonus Chapter

Amidst all my family fun, and before my son was born, New York's five boroughs were at the mercy of a serial killer. This terrorist put a real damper on dating for straight couples and in 1977 he finally identified himself as the *Son of Sam* by leaving a letter at one of his many crime scenes.

Most Latinos claimed to be un-phased by this threat. With a passion for life and our monopoly on lust, we laughed in the face of this danger. I was dating Willie but not exclusively, at least in my mind. He was still my metrosexual guy who kept my parents happy and who I could contend with, while I also dated girls. The joke amongst my friends was always that I as doubling my chances of getting murdered by this sicko who lurked our haunts after hours. Still, I shrugged it off. Mama walked around with a rosary in her house dress, ready to pray for Cenzo or me each time we walked out the door. "Don't appear to be dating" she should out every single time we left the house. The news was feeding us all the profile information and clearly, he was targeting couples.

I was either too young, too numb, or too dumb to be completely affected by Stacy Moskowitz's murder at the time, but this incident hit very close to home. Stacy and her sister Ricki were both friends of mine. I read the newspaper article to Willie with tears in my eyes while Mama tried to convince us to keep our dating to our backyard. "We have the barbeque and the pool right here and you don't have to go anywhere" she said, controlling her hysteria while holding the rosary beads in her hands. I tried to reach out to Ricki, but the news had descended on their household like vultures and their phone line was always busy. Neysa and Jerry, their parents were fixtures on New York television now; always shown crying or angry and ranting for Son of Sam's capture, at the time.

Stacy lived for 36 hours after being shot that fateful July evening. The world stood still in my house during that time with everyone in my family praying for her recovery. Her date was permanently blinded.

Willie was visibly affected by it all. He was an only child whole Mother had put the fear of Son of Sam firmly within his coconut. Mama reinforced his paranoia every time he mustered up the courage for us to go out, at my begging. I quickly grew tired of this and the constant focus we had put on this murderer, despite Stacy, but maybe for her too.

Mama and Cenzo called it stupid rebellion but I felt like he was always watching and gathering power from our fears. Too many Superhero comics and cartoons, perhaps, but this train of thought helped me to cope. While most of New York was besieged with fear and remaining indoors during one of the most beautiful summers of my life, I dated and danced a lot. Willie stayed home and perfected his Claymation techniques during this time, citing a burst of creative energy. I called him every time I went out and let him know once I had returned home safely.

While everyone lived in fear, I lived the wild and crazy native New Yorker way; unafraid and uninhibited. The temps were high that summer, so I took to wearing my brother's "A" t-shirts that I had grown to love, with baggy summer linen pants. I dressed for the islands and enjoyed island drinks like Piña Coladas and Margaritas during the summer of '77. I was tall and mature for my age, so I entered every club without being carded. I headed straight from the beach to Manhattan to party on Saturday, August 6th, in just such an outfit.

Ray was gorgeous inside and out. He was tanned, buff, sweet and safe. He was also openly bisexual. We grew up together and I was comfortable around him for all these reasons. We decided to trek to Manhattan together because he had discovered an "everything and everyone" club on west 72nd Street, with a summer happy hour and salsa to boot. Naidy, my current girl date, decided to join us on this adventure although she was not keen on my friendship with Ray.

We drank two for ones at the bar with a bunch of friendly cowboys that day and evening until the dance floor opened and the salsa music rocked the house. Ray was Columbian and a 'Salsero' extraordinaire. Naidy sat at the bar looking beautiful and getting more drinks purchased for her than any other woman could responsibly drink, so Ray and I helped her out.

The three of us were five hours into this club and drinking when Ray suggested that he and I exchange clothes. The crowd had thinned, and the air conditioning was never adjusted accordingly. I was sweating and freezing now on the dance floor in my little t-shirt. Ray was wearing a jean jacket, shirtless, with a peek-a-boo six pack teasing everyone in the crowd. He was hot, in every sense of the word. We made our way to the bathroom only to discover that it was one room for all, but we were young and brave. I removed my t-shirt and was half naked in front of Ray while he smiled and slowly removed his jacket. Other than keeping me in his view, he was the perfect gentleman throughout the exchange, but it was still hard to explain to Naidy when she walked in on us. It did not help that we were all so drunk. We staggered out of the club and headed for the train station with me now wearing the jean jacket, open down the middle, and Ray's cowboy hat too. Ray chaperoned us to just south of the train station but headed back to the club once I put my arm around Naidy. I explained the clothes exchange and we laughed, walking right past the train station, with our minds set on Chinese food before heading home. I remember saying how empty the streets were for a Saturday night before we say him walking towards us on Broadway.

He kept his hands in the pockets of a short creamy yellowish cotton jacket. His hair was curly, combed down, and he had piercing light eyes. Small and slightly overweight, he looked directly at my cleavage as he came upon Naidy and I, arm in arm. "What the fuck are you looking at?" I challenged him with. He was dorky and I was drunk. My female voice clearly confused him. The shock shown on his face. "I'm the Son of Sam" he said. Naidy and I laughed hard. Our guffaws echoed on the streets of Manhattan. We continued to walk past him as we did so, and he stopped to face us. I pulled a glass bottle out of the street trash can and threw it at him. It broke right in front of him and Naidy and I laughed our way to the Chinese take-out on west 77th Street.

I was on my way to school on August 11th of that following week when I stopped at the newspaper stand as part of my daily work week ritual. My knees buckled when I saw his face, wearing the creamy yellowish jacket, on the front of the New York Daily News. I ran to a pay phone and called Naidy immediately. We met later that day to read that edition from front to back page. Every picture of him, in various angles, confirmed that we had truly stood in front of David Berkowitz better known as the *'Son of Sam'*, that Saturday.

I have told this story in its entirety at many parties including the irony of him having killed my friend, to mixed reviews. It is 100% true. Naidy died, years later, so I have lost my one eye-witness.

Ray and I reminisced over beers many years later, in our thirties. He had killed many brain cells by that time and could not even remember this serial killer that plagues New York at that time.

He did remember by breasts when we exchanged clothes and my "Salsa Hips" when we danced.

About the Author

Joie Lamar is a Canadian citizen of Puerto Rican descent. She was born and raised in New York and made her way to Canada when she met the love of her life. They were married in Ontario after many years in a long distance relationship and have been together for over 21 years, at the time of this publication.

Mambo Lips is volume one of a two part memoir series and the beginning of Joie's writing adventure. Now a best selling author, with more published books to her portfolio, Ms. Lamar is passionate about 2SLGBTQ+ representation.

"This is an easy read novel sized for a day on the beach, park, or short rides on a train. It is not intended to be a long drawn out story of my life but simply an entertaining window view of me finding myself, and the family that made me who I am today!"

www.ingramcontent.com/pod-product-compliance
Lightning Source LLC
Chambersburg PA
CBHW030911080526
44589CB00010B/253